Wiley's Last Resort

Poems

Hilda Downer

REDHAWK
PUBLICATIONS

Redhawk Publications
The Catawba Valley Community College Press
2550 US Hwy 70 SE
Hickory NC 28602

ISBN: 978-1-952485-80-0

Library of Congress Control Number: 2022943232

Author Photo by Reba Tipton Vance

Cover Art by Robert Gipe

Cover Design by Shelly Benoit

Back Cover Photos by Scott Goebel

All photos used by permission.

"For anyone who didn't know Jim Webb, this book of fine poems is an apt biography. But not only is it a biography: it is equally something of a hagiography of the man once serio-comically addressed, in his most famous poem, as "Jesus." Reading these poems, we encounter the depth and breadth and persistence of Jim Webb's life and work—its sometimes terrible, awful, raging grace—and we see and hear what a secular Appalachian prophet and saint might look and sound like. For those who knew Jim for a long time, this book is the occasion of both joy and grief. We re-live him in his various guises and poses, hear his voice, watch his antics and his resistances, and we miss him.

For all readers, Hilda Downer's collection is a document of large love, devoted craft, and rich memories. There is really nothing like it in American poetry that I know of—an *Acts of the Apostle* of a complicated and flawed man, who lived a life at times of excess, and paid for it—spleen against greedheads and despoilers, among them most probably the arsonists who burned him out time after time, anger against injustice and abandonment—not only of human beings and their better angels, but of the land itself, given over to strip miners and mountain-top removers, which caused him deep suffering, and which engendered his vision and voice, reminiscent of the Beats.

But of all Jim Webb's excesses, the greatest of these were his generosity and love. They are reflected back into our lives through this sharp, true, totally unsentimental yet adoring book."

—Richard Hague, author of *During the Recent Extinctions: New & Selected Poems 1984-2012*

"*Wiley's Last Resort* is an affectionate tribute to the poet, activist, and radio personality Jim Webb. Hilda Downer, in poems vivid and compelling, celebrates Wiley Quixote (Webb), his dedication, voice, his fight against mountaintop removal, his inspiration to other poets, implicitly giving us fresh ways of seeing the contemporary Appalachian region and its people. Wiley Quixote is a person of contradictions and delight, remembered for his honesty, surprising energy, wit and generosity, love of community. He lives again in these poems."

—Robert Morgan, author of *Boone: A Biography*

"What a fine, poetic tribute Hilda Downer pays here to the late Jim Webb, iconic and iconoclastic Kentucky poet and raconteur. The poems include wide-ranging ruminations on art, poetry, and philosophy infused with a whimsy characteristic of Webb himself. That said, Downer does not neglect the gravitas with which Webb saw his role of painting an accurate portrait of Appalachia and its people, as well as his role as a combatant in the struggle to save the local environment. It's also impressive how these poems capture the essence of Webb's unremittingly zany re-naming of the world known as WILEY'S LAST RESORT, his camp-cum-conference center-cum demi-paradise there in south-eastern Kentucky. Nothing is missed in Downer's deftly poetic observations, not the "pink flamingo stakes," not even a discarded Emu! This is a fine book offering both a reverent and irreverent testimony to a man beloved by so many."

—Marc Harshman, Poet Laureate of West Virginia and author of *Woman in Red Anorak* (Blue Lynx Prize)

This book is dedicated to the Southern Appalachian Writers Cooperative, to Appalshop, to the caretakers and attendees of workshops at Highlander Research and Education Center and Hindman Settlement School, to the Appalachian Studies Association, and to Appalachian Voices for what these entities do for the Appalachian people and future generations. Also, to those who mourn the loss of beautiful brothers and sisters who are our heroes, to all who allow the mountains to ring forever, and to Reba.

Jim Webb with his father Watson Webb and Robb Webb, circa 1980.
Photo by Robb Webb.

In Memory of the Webb Brothers, Jim and Robb

"Robb was a candid, gracious, and generous man who admired his brother . . . 'I just hope people see Jim as a hero for all he's done. In fact, he is my hero.' Jim made the same comment about Robb many times over the years."

—Scott Goebel, "Remembering Founding Publisher Robb Webb"

"Jim's puns remain alive and well. His was a life of language in all its forms—the frontier tall tale, the Beat tradition blending the sacred and the profane, the earnest and the flippant, the punning naming of things—all in the service of truth and justice and art. His talk on the radio, his founding with his brother of *Pine Mountain Sand & Gravel*, the literary voice of the Southern Appalachian Writers Co-op, his good-natured quibbling and jesting among his friends, his burning vitriol cast at 'greedheads' and frauds—Jim created around himself a linguistic atmosphere in which the Word was always all."

—Richard Hague, "Dispatch From Wiley's Last Resort"

"The last time I saw Jim, it was pretty clear it was the last time I was going to see him. I kissed him on his forehead and said, 'Jim, you taught me everything I know.' He said, 'Then give me twenty dollars.' I wish I had."

—Robert Gipe, "Re: Wiley's Last Resort"

The author with Jim Webb at Jerry Wayne Williamson's retirement party, 2000.
Photo by Jan Hensley.

Introduction

Wiley Quixote is one of the pen names of the late Kentucky poet Jim Webb (September 24, 1945–October 22, 2018). Wiley is not just an imaginary proprietor of a real Appalachian campground, Wiley's Last Resort. Wiley is Jim Webb, and Jim Webb is Wiley, as the poet was a charismatic character unto himself, bigger than life. I make no pretense *not* to be referring to Jim Webb in these poems, which are about actual events propelled by the poet and the place. I mean only to use the name *Wiley* with fondness and in the spirit of friendly windmill jousting

Webb's being consisted of contradictions and equilibriums. Both extrovert and introvert, he also thought from both sides of his brain. He majored in biology and pre-med at Berea College and obtained a Master of Arts in English at Eastern Kentucky University. He taught English and Appalachian Studies at Southern West Virginia Community College, where—after the Great Central Appalachian Flood in 1977—he co-founded the Tug Valley Recovery Center to support relief and recovery efforts. He promoted local artists, musicians, community activists, and writers as a lifelong defender of the people and the mountains. Outspoken and comedic, he was Appalachia's resident genius. He was active with Kentuckians for the Commonwealth, Appalachian Voices, Appalachian Studies Association, Rotary Club, Letcher County Tourism Board, Letcher County Chamber of Commerce, Right Angle, and Otis Campbell Society.

Beyond his activism, Jim Webb's voice was widely known in the mountains from his writings and literary involvement. After the 1977 flood, he helped establish *The Sandy New Era*, the weekly newspaper where his commentaries under the pseudonym Wiley Quixote first appeared. It was during this time that he published with Bob Henry Baber the anthology *Mucked*, seen as a turning point in the nascent Appalachian Literary Renaissance. Webb was a founding member of the Southern Appalachian Writers Cooperative (SAWC) and a legendary swarper as well as the World's Greatest Flutophone Player. He founded the literary magazines *RECK* and *Pine Mountain Sand & Gravel* with his brother, Robb Webb (the announcer on

60 Minutes). His work appeared in numerous periodicals and anthologies, including *Appalachian Journal; Southern Exposure; Coal, a Poetry Anthology; Strokes; Old Wounds, New Words*; *Wild Sweet Notes: 50 Years of West Virginia Poetry,* and many others.

Wiley Quixote began his career as a radio personality in 1985 on WMMT-FM, the community radio component of Appalshop. His Wednesday program, *Ridin' Around Listenin' to the Radio with Wiley Quixote,* was heard around the "whirled." As production manager, he promoted many Appalachian musicians and writers with playlists and interviews.

Wiley's Last Resort, a primitive campground atop Pine Mountain in Letcher County, Kentucky, was formerly the old Pine Mountain Resort during Webb's childhood in the '40s and '50s, when he lived just across the road. The property was defunct and run down by the time Webb acquired it. He began restoration in 1996, starting with the spring-fed lake (Walled-in Pond), and designated campsites throughout the magical 80 acres of rare flora and fauna. He began to host several annual events, such as environmentalist group meetings and concerts on a solar-powered stage. Wiley's Last Resort, for several years, was designated for SAWC the weekend before or after the nearby Writers' Workshop at Hindman Settlement School. (SAWC also met annually to read and present at the Appalachian Studies Association Conference at Highlander in New Market, Tennessee, and at the Seedtime on the Cumberland Festival in Whitesburg, Kentucky.) Many members of SAWC also attended other events at Wiley's Last Resort. A highlight was the infamous Annual Pine Mountain Tacky Lawn Ornament and Pink Flamingo Soiree, held since 1985 during the full moon every August. Wiley's Last Resort was a refuge for lone writers like me to huddle over a notebook in the woods or to hike to Bad Branch Falls. There was no charge to stay at the campground—only donations and barter were accepted.

Due to his activism, Webb lost three homes to fire, allegedly by arson. The first was the home place that he and his brother had inherited. The other two were at Wiley's Last Resort. Although Webb suffered a complete loss with each fire, his countless friends helped him pick up the pieces and move on, with more determination than ever. To this day, his voice cannot be silenced, even after death.

Webb's poem, "Get In, Jesus," published in the early 1980s in a college text edited by Tom McLaughlin at Appalachian State University, catapulted him to stardom among Appalachian writers and scholars. This iconic narrative poem recalls Webb's experience while hitchhiking during the '70s with long hair and a beard. Although the poem is self-deprecating, it is hard for the reader not to compare Webb's selfless struggle to stop strip mining and mountaintop removal with the actions of the biblical Jesus. (For SAWCers, the acronym WWJD stands for What Would Jim Do.) At poetry readings, Webb sold his classic, "Get In, Jesus," literary T-shirt in different colors and editions. His sole book, *Get In, Jesus*—consisting of poetry, satirical essays, and musings—was not published until 2013, by Wind Publications. SAWC member Scott Goebel painstakingly searched through everything from notes written on paper plates to archives of libraries to compile the collection. A mother lode of poems was discovered in a desk drawer, kept safe at the *Appalachian Journal,* by Webb's friend and former editor of *AJ*, Jerry Wayne Williamson.

My own poems here reflect my humble attempt to depict real experiences with an imaginary man, Wiley Quixote, that either I witnessed, a friend witnessed, or Webb told me himself. There are so many stories that each poet in SAWC could write a poem, or already has, concerning Jim (including how he came to get the nickname Ski King, and other topics I don't even broach). Even the stories I do write about are not my stories. They belong to SAWC, his many friends and coworkers, and family. Moreover, they belong to Webb—as Webb belongs to us in fleeting moments throughout infinity. As the creator of "Get In, Jesus," proprietor of Wiley's Last Resort for the benefit of the community, and activist for the environment and the Appalachian people, Jim Webb may be as close to an Appalachian holy man as we will ever witness.

Hilda Downer

Acknowledgements

The author gratefully acknowledges the following journals
in which these poems have appeared:

Pine Mountain Sand & Gravel

"Wiley's Voice"

"12 Poems" (as "18 Poems")

"Wiley Looks Like He's Famous"

"Wiley Goes to the Highest Peak"

"Wiley's Silver Cap in My Lap"

"Wiley Takes T-shirt Inventory"

Avant Appal(achia) 2018

"*Route 23 North* (Painting by Jeff Chapman-Crane)"

"The Lyrebird"

Table of Contents

In Memory of the Webb Brothers, Jim and Robb   7

Introduction   9

Stay A-Wiley at the Top of the Whirled   **17**

Wiley Gives the Full Tour   19

First Time Camping at Wiley's   23

Near New York City on the Wiley's Last Resort Map   26

Flood Stage at Wiley's Last Resort   27

Wiley Takes T-shirt Inventory   30

The Emu   32

Wiley's Former Girlfriend Hides Out   34

Appalachian Howl   37

Skinny Dipping at Walled-in Pond   44

Appalachian Frankenstein   47

Route 23 North (Painting by Jeff Chapman-Crane)   50

Wiley Invites Jeff to Supper   53

Appalachian Voices   **57**

Wiley's Voice   59

Wiley's "Get In, Jesus" Poem   60

Wiley Reads His America Poem   61

Wiley Looks Like He's Famous   64

Making a Living with Their Voices   66

Be Purple   67

Party for Wiley's Girlfriend   69

SAWC Gathering at Highlander   71

Wiley Tells the History of Highlander   72

Highlander Group Photo   73

The Delbert Awards at Highlander   74

Chartreuse   75

Poultry in Motion   77

Wiley Quixote Says Grace   78

Pioneer Stereo   80

Bob Henry Offers an Art Class at the ASA Conference   81

The Confessional   82

The Arrow   84

Pink Flamingos in Kentucky   86

12 Poems   88

Wiley Says He'll Never Write a Novel   90

Music to Life   92

Goose Creek Symphony   94

Unlike Greedheads, Wiley Says He's a Varlet   95

Wiley Says He Doesn't Want to Be Tied Down   97

Wiley's Silver Cap in My Lap   101

Wiley Goes to the Highest Peak   102

Wiley Flees Coal Company Security   104

Wiley's Heart Is in the Right Place   106

Note to Wiley   108

Wiley Attends Hindman Writers' Workshop at Night   110

Vinyl Record   113

Wiley's Cache   116

The Lyrebird   119

Travel Mugs   121

Five Words   124

Wiley Came In and Went Out with the Hunter's Moon   126

Footnote to Wiley's Last Resort   128

Works Cited   131

Bibliography   133

Author's Special Thanks   134

Previously Published by Hilda Downer   135

About the Author   137

Sand Bar(d) Gorilla at night.
Photo by Malcom Wilson.

Stay A-Wiley at the Top of the Whirled

When I told (Wiley) about Jesus and the wine . . .
he had enough pilgrims as it was, he said,
who come looking not for miracles or salvation,
but to quench a thirst for oblivion's cousin.
Sooner or later everyone arrived at his last resort.
'They'll have to bring their own inspiration.'

— David Wayne Hampton, "Whiskey or Wine"

. . . where chinks have fallen from logs
—license for misguided vines—
to wrap around beams, to exit again to light.

—Bob Henry Baber, "Heirs"

I have accepted lying
the hours awake until first light.
But I've come to love the whippoorwill again,
the echo and rustle in quiet woods,
the folds and snags in familiar quilts,
new opportunities,
roots,
and rain.

—Ann Shurgin, "First Night in a New Bed"

. . . and morning
tawdry as ever, rubs against the mountains,
burnishing them like old copper pots,
dented and familiar . . .

—Edwina Pendarvis, "Appalachian Aubade #2"

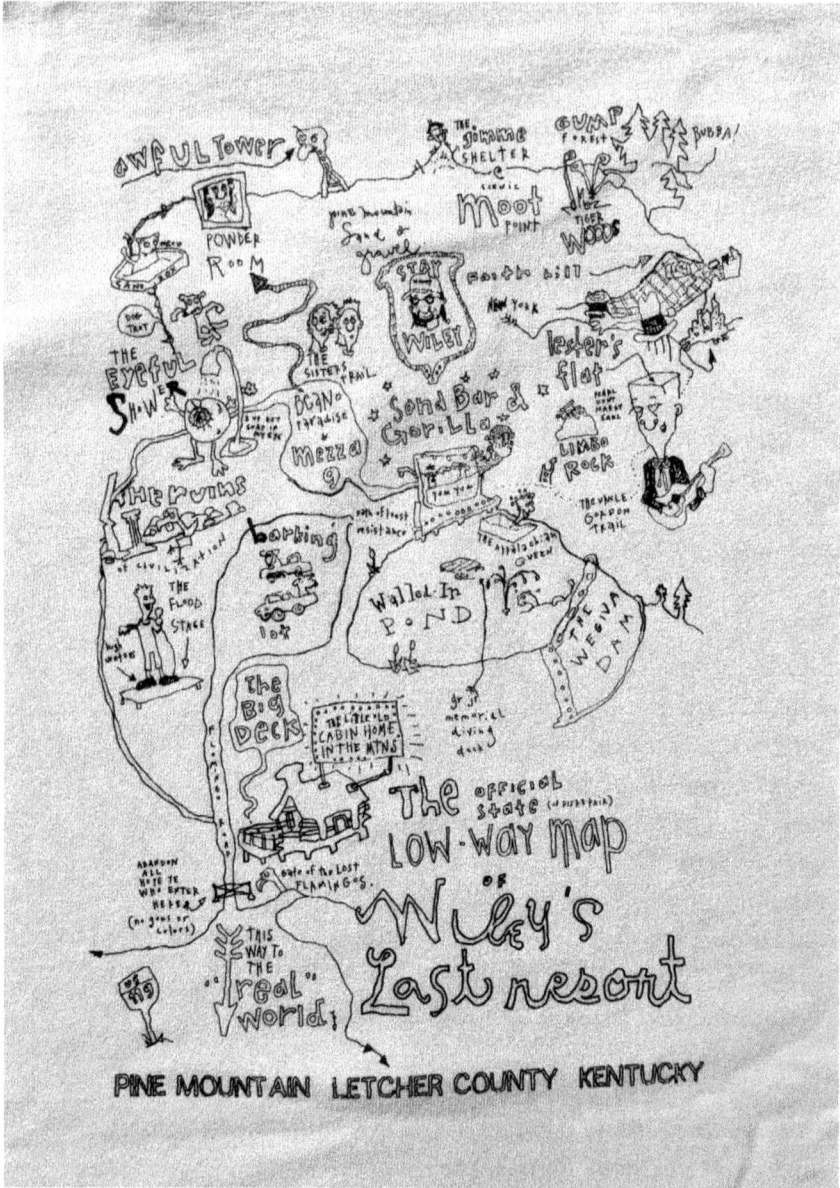

"Wiley's Last Resort Map" T-shirt design by Robert Gipe.
Photo by Steven Justice.

Wiley Gives the Full Tour

Take a walk on the wild side.

Take a walk with Wiley—

not a trip around the Whirled in 90 days,

not a three-hour tour,

just walk awhile with Wiley

up and down Wiley's Last Resort.

Starting at the Sand Bar(d) Gorilla,

go past Walled-in Pond

where Cardinal flowers anoint the water's edge.

Take this walk near dusk

as woods rehearse daylight's final revision

of the breeze moving constellations through leaves.

Chuckle at the regulatory signs,

Stay a-Wiley, and, *We giva dam,*

with drawings of a beer bottle and a PBR can,

the bottle X'd through—

no glass allowed.

After a swarp, Wiley stomped the cans for recycling

until his first use of the hand press, he called a "press rehearsal."

The first campsite, donned New York,

is where Brother Robb

camps when he comes home

from New York City.

Bordered by Tiger Woods, Lester's Flat

faces Black Mountain—

coal-busy machine lights,

disruptive as the buzz of a hornet's nest.

Wiley sighs, *Twenty-four hours a day.*

On the crest of Gump Forest

is the lone writer's retreat.

St. Elmo's Haven

adorns the slender dirt road,

Stairway to Haven,

like a ring dangling on the tip of a finger.

Climb up Faith Hill

to land on MARS,

where excavation exposed

swirls of red sand—

proof Kentucky was once under the sea.

Wiley has given the full tour countless times.

Yet, his guest feels

this is the first time Wiley has shared

his enthusiasm for the land he loves.

Wiley's greatest talent,

maybe more than crafting words,

might be making each person he talks to

feel special.

He veers up rock steps

on the Path to Enlightenment

to a huge boulder

called Stoned Henge

where guests can imbibe—

an overlook of the lake.

Future plans are disclosed—

to install a fountain to aerate

for the quality of the water

and the health of aquatic life.

Past the Powder Room,

the Two Sisters Path through woods

leads to the hose stretched under full sun,

solar warmth for outdoor showers in the open—

the Eyefull Shower.

To the right is Roger's camper,

dubbed The Rajmahal.

On the way down to the Barking Lot,

gather tinder on the edge

of woods filling with darkness

from the bottom like a Mr. Coffee pot.

That red demonic blinking in the sky

is the Awful Tower—

the cell tower on Wiley's Last Resort

that he shrugs off regret

because he gave permission—

wanting to help neighbors.

The campfire is produced by SAWC,

firewood gathered by the touch of the poets—

Scott, Dana, Mike, Ann, Dick,

David, Beto, and Jim.

The fire crackles a geyser of embers—

warm ground and cooling night,

the thermal conduction of stories told here.

Those who have walked with Wiley

think about where they've been.

First Time Camping at Wiley's

It was part of Wiley's humorous nomenclature

on the map of Wiley's Last Resort—

a campsite called New York in rural Kentucky.

Wiley tells campers they can camp

anywhere on the resort

except in New York City.

That sacred site is reserved for his brother.

Out of respect,

we stamp out a place just below—

more like New Jersey on a folding travel map.

Location is everything at Wiley's.

We are close enough to the Swarp

yet far enough not to be kept awake.

A fallen oak makes a handy bench.

A rhododendron becomes a closet with open arms

to display vintage prom dresses.

A red bandana tied to a sapling stakes our claim,

pays homage to coal miners who fought for rights,

and honors my childhood in Bandana.

It's been a long time

since I set up a tent.

With Ann's expertise,

she isn't fooled long

as I measure the tent bottom

right out of the bag.

Then, I mark the ground

to drive the pink flamingo stakes.

Ann gently demonstrates putting the tarp

on the ground first and the tent on top of that.

It's coming back to me.

We insert rods from opposite sides

that cross on top—

another X for God to see.

Assembled,

the tent sags like a fallen cake.

Giggling, we take photos of ourselves

in front of the lopsided tent

before starting over.

Pulled toward the campfire—

Mike on the mandolin

and Wiley on the flutophone—

we join the singing

of "Which Side Are You On?"

We are where we want to be

with those we want to be with,

more than anywhere else in the Whirled—

a SAWC gathering

at Wiley's Last Resort.

Near New York City on the Wiley's Last Resort Map

Throughout the deep night,

the air mattress

slowly exhales until fully compressed.

A rock nudges its knife into Ann's rib.

My back against the ground

becomes a rough-sawn plank.

We don't know

the other is awake

when a whippoorwill cuts through darkness—

hauntingly rare,

not heard since childhood.

Whippoorwill, whippoorwill

stitches a silver thread

straight through our souls—

holds in place the fabric of fog

curled paisley over Walled-in Pond.

Now, I can pin this call

as the moment

our friendship began,

built on separate joy,

unspoken,

to share and revisit over the years.

Flood Stage at Wiley's Last Resort

On the road to Damascus,
Gentry Creek threw its leg over the bank
to wrestle the road to its level.
Firefighters on the other side
encouraged us to drive across—
Red Rover. Red Rover,
my red Subaru seemed to gingerly lift its skirt,
cartoonish, as it stepped into fast water.
They waved frantically to STOP
as a tree floated by.
Again, they motioned us onward.

Finally arrived at Wiley's,
sealed jugs of water stood intact
on my car's soaked floorboard.
Ann and I sent a glance
of fright to each other—
the recognition
that the creek had been high enough
to drag us under its stampede.

We camped nearby other SAWCers—
fire stamped out by steady rain.
Rain that followed us from Boone,
through Tennessee and Virginia,

would not let up all weekend.

Dana said downpours all the way

from Georgia made the drive through Hell.

Drenched sleeping bags draped chairs

under the mercy of a plastic roof,

half walls, only a gesture against incoming torrents,

at the Sand Bar(d) Gorilla.

Wiley's dryer ran like a gerbil, night and day,

with damp jeans and plaid shirts.

The new inflated mattress kept us above

water inching up our tent floor,

but a few tents caved in from the pressure

and sank to their knees.

My notebook began to bleed out—

folded over, limp.

Constant hard rain and Wiley

started the tempo for each day

by egging on a big breakfast.

We talked about poems even as we ate.

Ann finished washing the dishes

while Scott and I remained

talking about our poetry lives,

enhanced by having children.

Ever the good host,

Wiley started off the morning

workshop for miserable souls,

Welcome to the Zen way of workshopping!

His laughter set us at ease even as we shivered.

Cold settled into the bones

of concrete walls that tenderly wept.

I had mistakenly made brownies with cake mix

but all got eaten anyway

as Wiley offered warm blankets—

so well-versed at disaster relief

after strip mining caused floods.

Wiley became his own "Mr. Flood's Party,"

singing against all adversity,

ever grateful for a swarp of writers,

and the refuge of a clear plastic roof—

all that separated us from the wrath of God.

Wiley knew this, too, shall pass.

His parables were by example:

tiny seeds beaten down into mud—

all they needed to hunker down

to make the best of a bad situation

for their future bugle cry

of yellow and pink—

Dutchman's Breeches and Ladyslippers.

Wiley Takes T-shirt Inventory

Two medium Soirees in pink,

one purple extra, extra large Soiree,

three large long-sleeved natural Jesuses,

one medium natural Jesus,

one black Jesus in large,

four little red Jesuses—

yellow Jesuses have yet to come out.

Wiley recognizes and shakes his head *no*

to his colorful count

that could be misinterpreted as racial slurs—

intolerance not tolerated

at the all-inclusive

Wiley's Last Resort.

A car screeches the sharp curve.

Wiley faults engineers of the new road construction

for the wreck of a chlorine truck

and potential spill into Walled-in Pond.

Speaking of albino fish, he jests

and recalls blind salamanders in the spring cave.

How are your eyes anyway?

He looks straight at me

above an old photograph of Wiley's Last Resort

before the fires put out the tourists.

All I can see is Black Mountain

offering itself to our distance

and a coal company

erasing Kentucky's highest peak.

Comprehension cannot inventory

whole mountains spread to eviscerate

or lampshades made from human skin—

Wars, whores, pieces of silver and gold.

How do I explain true evil to my sons,

Appalachian sons,

mute against a defaced mountain?

And it was good—

so rare I can say this of what I create,

except for these two.

One son sports a new black Jesus.

The other dons a faded verdant one.

I clutch black fabric rich as any coal beneath

and hold onto the other like Heaven's green earth,

holding on

to stand up.

Stand up. Stand up for Jesus.

The Emu

It comes up sometimes
during a SAWC gathering.
Were you there when The Emu jumped out?

The highway atop the steep bank
above Wiley's Last Resort
is strategic for tossing the unwanted—
fast-food debris,
the non-biodegradable,
and puppies.

We were all in agreement with Dick
who said Scott's poem would work better
by switching the first and last stanzas
when the sudden halt of a van caught our attention.

The driver got out, ran to the back,
opened the door, ran back to the front,
jumped in, and drove off.

There stood The Emu.

Wiley had been expecting another
three-legged Jack to join his fleet
of mongrels set out this way.
Give Wiley your huddled masses,
your tired, your poor emu.

Later that summer,

I camp with my sons at Wiley's,

doubting The Emu is still there.

Out of the woods, a scene straight from Jurassic Park,

the forbidding bird approaches, taller than sons.

I instruct firmly as during a Code Blue,

No sudden moves.

I see my children living in the moment,

palms outstretched with laughter and granola—

no regret, no fear of the future,

only the wonderment

of The Emu stepping from shadow,

another dimension,

just for them.

I can see myself flipping through the rolodex

of genetic experience for what to do

when faced with prehistoric artillery—

hard beak, eviscerating claws,

and powerful legs that can outrun at 30 mph.

I can see my living in the moment

already includes what I am saving

for later

in order to search for

and write down

my answer.

I was there.

Wiley's Former Girlfriend Hides Out

Everything went as usual or unusual

as at any SAWC event.

Wiley told no one she was there

but, once, her voice trailed over Walled-in Pond

and Wiley glanced toward the cabin.

Before he ate his own breakfast,

he carefully piled high a second plate—

gravy and biscuits

including at least one of each fresh or fried item.

As though no one would notice

his not speaking a word,

he veered toward the cabin.

He upheld the flimsy paper plate,

despite his hand tremor—

neurological, never from stage fright.

He stumbled once on gravel,

recovered quickly—

the plate raised upright like the Eucharist.

I suddenly believed that love could last forever.

She had escaped rehab,

barely out of withdrawals.

Why not prescribe painkillers to the likes of us?

After all, what better things do we have to do?

Wiley wrote defiantly in a poem.

She was safe at Wiley's

and he had a plan—

his lawyer forever on standby.

Wiley's poem raged

about his defense of her in court.

Her small son doesn't need her

so, of course, she's better off in jail.

Rilke's terrible angels

and the wrath of God,

there is still so much beauty.

The voice that carried across the lake

was the liquid mystery of dark blue

tinged with feminine pain.

Alone in the cabin,

hiding from the law,

bearing our laughter,

watching our fires,

she waited as one does

the night before execution.

She could not know

she would be off opiates for good,

hold down a job,

get her son back,

or spark a Wiley poem.

In that vacancy of dread,

she gathered her strength in the cabin mirror,

flanked by stick-on flamingos,

trying to be fierce

as the snake tattoo

around her neck.

Appalachian Howl

(after Allen Ginsberg)

Just as I am without one plea,

I come. We come.

We come, carrying scuffed guitars

and old fiddles like black walnuts

cracked out of seasoned shells.

We come accompanied

with moonshine jars and crumpled poems.

We come, stuffed in backseats of 4WDs,

from our cabins in the laurels and hollers

or trailers set up in front of old home places:

dripping from a sea-journey on the

highway across America.

We come from growing up with a shouting preacher

so frightening we thought he was drunk.

We place dahlias on family graves at Decoration,

put up pickled corn and beets,

camp along remote trails near the Appalachian Trail,

and long for hound dogs in swept dirt yards.

Some come with gratitude for an orange,

a peppermint stick,

or an apple stack cake only at Christmas.

Others had parents move off for work,

the station wagon loaded every weekend

to return home, to the mountains.

We come with Bluegrass, Country, Blues, Classical,

Rock 'n' Roll, Reggae, Jazz, Hip Hop, and audio books

trailing our vehicles as we drive in—

a perfume of sound.

By the time we get to Wiley's,

we're a couple hundred strong.

Wiley, thoroughly swarping,

wears a stuffed flamingo hat

while running everything

smooth as molasses on a buttered biscuit.

"Get In, Jesus" and Soiree T-shirts abound,

but I prefer a vintage prom dress and cowgirl boots,

mindful of copperheads this time of year.

Wiley wears his gold dinner jacket.

He's easy to spot as his own light,

day or night.

Attendance is by invitation only—

a pink slip in the mail—

except for the multimedia artist

headed out West from Manhattan,

beckoned by multi-colored Christmas lights,

stops by out of curiosity.

Dancing an Irish jig with new friends on the dock,

he's glad he did.

We come for round-the-clock

bands and poetry readings

on the Solar Stage—

> the / poem is holy the voice is
>
> holy the hearers are holy
>
> the ecstasy is holy!

Flamingos, in every pose and size,

fashioned out of fabric, wood, plastic, and metal

are painted, sewn, or welded.

Flamingos, everywhere, stop us in their tracks.

We come for the after-midnight jam cruise

on the "Pontune," also dubbed the Appalachian Queen,

decked with solar lights.

Scott jokes, *Now, Ann, you don't get this in Waller, Texas!*

Here, at Wiley's Last Resort,

I see the best minds of my generation:

>   *Holy the supernatural extra*

>   *brilliant intelligent kindness of*

>   *the soul!*

As filmmakers, journalists,

radio announcers, sportswriters,

activists, environmentalists,

the movers and the makers,

the salt and the shakers,

the canoers on the lakers,

we come.

From every campsite comes a generous offer.

Uncle Raymond calls out,

Want to try rattlesnake—

free range, and naturally rodent fed?

Marlene adds a slice of bread

from sourdough starter kept alive for generations

and homemade wine from heirloom grapes:

bodies! suffering! magnanimity!

In every molecule of this soil on Pine Mountain,

there is a universe.

When coal companies remove mountains,

they remove the headwaters,

the flora and fauna;

the people and their culture.

We call that genocide.

Some of us nearly destroyed by opiates,

we come back to ourselves

to meet on that distant shore.

We come,

tromped on,

burned out, gaumed up,

hoodooed, hog-tied,

tarred and feathered,

lawyered, thieved from,

and held under the gun.

We come to stand as one.

I am with you at Wiley's.

Our tents mushroom the woods,

I am with you at Wiley's.

An open fire as our flag of unity,

I am with you at Wiley's.

We come as hairdressers and nurses.

I am with you at Wiley's.

Scholars, singers, and farmers, we come.

I am with you at Wiley's.

Having eaten cornbread and pinto beans all our lives,

I am with you at Wiley's.

We come. We connect the future to our forebears:

   Holy forgiveness! mercy!

   charity! faith! Holy! Ours!

When the full moon presses its fingertip

onto the page of midnight,

silence strains

the dark rooms of our ears

for a remote giggle or cough.

Wiley signals it's time.

All howl at the moon.

The moon beams approval,

and the lake rolls out its native tongue,

the welcome mat

to God's cabin door

during the Annual Pine Mountain

Tacky Lawn Ornament

and Pink Flamingo Soiree

at Wiley's Last Resort.

Skinny Dipping at Walled-in Pond

Awakened by lines I need to write,

careful not to disturb Ann

on the same air mattress,

I slip out my silken sleeping bag—

emerge from the tent like a butterfly.

I'm up earlier than anyone at the reggae event—

alone to love the sign language of fog over the lake—

until the woods discharge a group of young men

where the exhausted campfire smolders.

After a long night of music and drinking,

they're still enjoying themselves.

One of them is especially friendly,

Hey, come and go skinny dipping with us.

I smile and thank him

but say I must decline this time.

He promises not to look.

That's good, I say in an attempt to pull rank,

because I am older than your granny.

The young man and his laughing buddies won't quit.

Hey, I'll let you look at mine.

I think you'll be impressed.

44

The eternal smiley one chimes in,

I'll even let you touch mine.

That does it.

I really doubt that, I say.

As a nurse, I have catheterized

enough males not to be easily impressed.

Wiley approaches, within earshot.

He gives me a quick warning glance.

I've never seen that look of his before.

Wiley prides himself that at Wiley's Last Resort,

there has never been a broken bottle—

never a fight.

Before the settlers arrived,

Kentucky was a common hunting ground,

a place of peace.

Wiley announces *Good Morning,*

bright as a radio alarm.

Young men skitter into water.

In his "Get In, Jesus" poem,

the possibility of being crucified

by crazed drunks

transforms into a humorous outcome,

a miracle.

I feel ashamed

of becoming angry

at foolish play,

not turning it around;

of having to be rescued.

No one had to rescue Wiley.

No one rescued Jesus.

Appalachian Frankenstein

Wiley and what judges he could muster

peruse campsites

to choose the Tackiest Lawn Ornament in the competition

of the Annual Pine Mountain Tacky Lawn Ornament

and Pink Flamingo Soiree.

Wiley was clear in the pink invitation—

whoever wins has to take the prize.

Anything goes, from a Bathtub Santa

to a toilet flower pot.

A looming papier-mâché bear is bemused

by the disparity of pink flamingos bantering too close.

Appalachian Frankenstein

is a loser on Faith Hill—

his dilapidated hat, the color of dirt.

Real tobacco juice

from the entry of his corn cob pipe

drips down a corn silk beard.

His ribcage, a radiator,

could repurpose into a lethal still.

His camouflage jacket

rattles with shotgun shells.

These campers deride

Hollywood stereotypes of us—

one leg shorter than the other.

Why didn't they make a bride?

Perhaps I would do—

laced up in a maxi dress,

stomping around in brogans,

hair frizzy as broom sedge in the wind.

Water falling over the dam of Walled-in Pond

could be my white veil.

He is more frightened than frightening

with no voice in the matter.

I can see his creators want to help

the miners and the environment

as he stares out from a life not worth living—

toward Black Mountain, beheaded for coal

also formed of dead things—

though he is at a great party.

The Statue of Liberty is the sure-fire winner!

She's drop-dead gorgeous,

mummified in duct tape

(called Carolina Chrome back home).

Wiley entertains my suggestion

that Lady Liberty should be

Appalachian Frankenstein's bride.

After all, her flame is alive

with battery-operated candles

sunk into yellow and orange plastic flowers—

upheld like a bridal bouquet

in mid toss.

Wiley quickly jumps in,

Would they have Appalach-younguns?

I don't even have to spell it out for him,

Their daughter would be named Appalajane.

His laughter is tinctured

with the recognition of my loneliness.

He understands that we all

have a cross to bear,

that, tonight, humor is the only recompense

for the hardship

of those who lived before us.

Route 23 North

(Painting by Jeff Chapman-Crane)

Looking like Jesus is only half the battle.

At Wiley's Last Resort,

the Walled-in Pond

may not turn into wine

but it does reflect moon shine.

Jesus is the Word,

and *Victory* is a word

not meant for mortals to comprehend.

Wiley bought Jeff's painting with monthly installments.

He liked that Jeff left the telephone lines

that cross the street scene of Jenkins—

the way it can be seen from Route 23 North,

headed toward more lucrative jobs.

Everything lost in Wiley's first fire—

Jeff used the same photograph

to reproduce the original.

Other donations of appliances,

housewares, and pink flamingos

framed an identical painting of Jenkins.

Jeff uses egg tempera,

pigments mixed with egg yolk,

instead of his own blood as the painters of old.

Those of us without special powers

cannot register the detail of one blade of grass

growing out of Jeff's emulsion.

We can only smell its sharp green,

rough against our lips.

Standing on the roadside of Route 23,

we might notice exterior brickwork,

even movement in its pattern

of dark magenta fading toward brown,

but Jeff's painting causes us to remember

what we never saw—

light finally visible

from a star that no longer exists.

Jeff charges extra for hands,

the hardest of all for him to paint.

Yet, effortlessly, he reflects love

in the brown eyes of his wife's portrait.

(Wiley mused that praying hands,

viewed from one side,

should only be half price.)

While in art school, my son

debated that a painting

should not look exactly like the subject,

Why not just take a photograph?

I argued that a painting and a photograph

each holds its own spirit and truth.

In Jeff's paintings and Wiley's poems,

Jesus, himself, must have walked

across the lines,

transformed into life lines

neither painter nor poet

could have intended—

where destructive flames

cannot hold down

new life already waving freely

from within.

Wiley Invites Jeff to Supper

Mind you, when Wiley

is invited to the gallery for breakfast,

Jeff makes crepes,

wondrous with a color wheel of toppings,

including homemade peach ice cream

cranked out by the artist himself.

When Jeff arrives,

Wiley offers him an adult beverage—

PBR because Wiley doesn't like the way

other beer companies treat the environment.

Wiley puts supper on.

It's quite a production, Jeff notices,

with all the elaborate preparation

of Wiley opening a can of Dinty Moore Beef Stew.

While most of the major food groups simmer,

Wiley tidies up.

Aiming a small yogurt container

toward the pail for plastics,

he inspects it first—

the kind with an aluminum foil tab that pulls off.

Why this isn't good for nothing,

he shakes his head with all the despair

of a mother bird in a nest full of mites.

They carry chairs to the lake.

Their lives depend on food, water, shelter,

and art—the joy of life

that causes them

to come in out of the rain

to eat, drink, and be merry.

What do these great minds

ponder on this pinnacle of evenings?

No recordings of Wordsworth and Coleridge

gazing across mountain lakes

while hiking through Scotland,

Jeff and Wiley's conversation

plucks the lake surface—

to ring outward as whole notes

into the music of the spheres.

Jeff will be left to remember

these moments on this island of time,

PBRs safely wedged in the grass,

no place to rest his bowl of stew

except on the imaginary last supper table

at Wiley's Last Resort.

Stoned Flamingo mosaic by Jeff Chapman-Crane.
Photo by Scott Goebel or Nelson Pilsner.

Appalachian Voices

Lord, how our voices often mingle,
creeks rounding down from a thousand miles
to wed the same bright river
And how we mouth our favorite names:
say poplar, sycamore, broom sedge
like prayers . . .

—Richard Hague, "Talking Together"

Something in me stirs, comes out of hiding
like rabbits slipping from fields in the evening.
And whatever was crushed in me straightens slowly
now like grass after it has been walked on.

—Jim Wayne Miller, "Three Days of Rain"

I come into the presence of still water.
And I feel above me the day-blind stars
Waiting with their light. For a time
I rest in the grace of the world, and am free.

—Wendell Berry, "The Peace of Wild Things."

Bob Dylan Birthday Party, Wiley's Last Resort, 2016.
Photo by Malcolm Wilson.

Wiley's Voice

This is the powder room

where they stored dynamite,

he spoke, stepping out of the concrete vault,

as the reverb of his voice inside

overlapped his voice outside.

Both voices closed so sharply

that I noticed the emptiness

of space

and what it must be like

to love someone who dies before you.

Driving back from Kentucky

I find his radio show on WMMT, 88.7.

Distance begins to rust the voice,

more powerful than the powder

required to explode a mountain for coal.

Losing reception,

I listen to the static of silence

that I remember from before I was born

as the sound of infinity.

Wiley's "Get In, Jesus" Poem

It's a running joke among SAWCers.

When one of us pulls up in a car,

you hold out your thumb,

and the driver says, *Get in, Jesus.*

Jim Webb at SAWC gathering at
Highlander, 2013.
Photo by Beto Cumming.

Wiley Reads His America Poem

Walled-in Pond serves as background

for our lawn chairs beside the Sand Bar(d) Gorilla.

Wiley's picturesque log cabin,

living quarters after the second fire,

punctuates the other side of the lake.

Wiley shuffles up to the podium.

A few giggles spread.

He's funny just standing there.

He says *America* to begin his America poem.

We are hanging onto every mountain

enunciation etched onto our souls

by ancestors who fled oppression.

Wiley pauses.

He stares into the distance.

We all turn,

watch in silent reverence—

three deer walk beside us,

skirt the lake, and enter the woods.

Wiley resumes reading his America poem.

Wiley's Last Resort is on top of Pine Mountain,

the second highest peak in Kentucky.

Wiley wants to keep it that way,

but the coal company keeps hacking away

at Black Mountain

as we sleep, as we wake.

You don't know what he is going to say,

but you know it's going to be brilliant.

Burned out three times,

he lands on his feet again.

His America poem

addresses big coal companies.

Wiley's voice booms,

shakes the rafters of the woods,

You sorry, sorry Greedheads!

He tells them, once and for all,

to stop pillaging the mountains.

That is, if any one of them likes to drink water—

leave the headwaters alone.

When he gives a final radical yell,

collective tears sting and we squeeze hands

with those beside us.

Scott shouts, *Come on now, Wiley.*
Tell us how you really feel!

Wiley tells a story.

When he first started

reading his *poultry* against strip mining,

a heated woman in the audience

opposed his use of expletives.

She called him an angry young man.

Well, he explained,

It's like when you lose at shooting pool.

You don't just say, 'Shucky darn.'

Wiley Looks Like He's Famous

Wiley wakes up like anyone

to urinate outside

when the gravity water pipe is occluded

by a salamander or daisy.

Just like the next guy,

he extricates himself from a pink flamingo iron gate

to go to work

at the Seedtime Festival on the Cumberland.

Somewhere in the streaming sunlight

between a busy schedule and bronchitis,

he manages to sit down.

A camera crew approaches.

One of them sums it up,

You look like you're famous.

He is renowned

for his "Get In, Jesus" poem on T-shirts

sold in an array of exciting colors,

25 bucks a pop,

but they don't know that.

They just want answers,

and luck out getting Wiley Quixote—

just like me,

sitting next to the Master of Ceremonies.

Naturally, we talk about Jesus

over barbecue and moonshine.

The barbecue makes Wiley think of roadkill

and dying for the sins of others.

He proclaims Jesus was an eloquent speaker

or nobody would have listened to him say shit.

That's all I need for the rest of the day,

the inertia to keep thinking

about God parting the waters open as a library dictionary.

Wiley's Last Resort mined for sand,

Walled-in-Pond was once the ocean.

When Jesus walked on water,

he made all the waters one.

A ripple reaches us now.

A purified droplet balms

a foreign shore of war.

Where they dammed mountain streams into a lake,

even the draining of Appalachia is power.

Making a Living with Their Voices

Wiley's brother is the announcer on *60 minutes*

This is 60 minutes.

It sounds made up

as the name, Wiley Quixote—

someone from Appalachia

making it big and living in New York City.

It's true though.

That rich laden voice belongs to Robb.

Wiley just wants stereotypes to stop.

He shows the diversity of mountain people

on his radio show.

We're not all from Scotland.

We're from Africa, Asia, Europe, South America . . .

and already here, Native American.

We are here.

Wiley has a small TV in the cabin,

no cable that far out.

Robb mails tapes of shows.

Wiley watches one

when he feels homesick

for his brother's voice.

Be Purple

Someone who didn't know Wiley

could figure out who he was

by the way he *favored* his people.

Why you're the spitting image of your Grandpap.

Lord, you're all growed up!

He sat on the porch swing

sipping spring water handed to him

in a jelly jar with flowers,

dark shades of purple and blue.

He declined the customary offer of food,

not wanting to be any trouble,

though pork chops, collard greens, mashed taters,

sliced maters, salted cucumbers, and cornbread

sounded *awful* good.

He just went ahead and popped the question.

Myrtle was flabbergasted.

Asked to be a weekly host for an hour on WMMT

was not what she was expecting,

but Wiley liked to include the community.

Why I don't know nothing about no radio, she objected.

Neither do we, Wiley laughed.

With another convert to help spread

music and the word,

Wiley walked away carrying a big poke

of maters and squash from her garden.

Myrtle waved, calling after him, *Be careful,*

heard all his life on departure

in the mountain dialect

that, as a child,

he thought people were saying, *Be purple.*

He drove off, astonished

about the power of sound.

Once the church bell rings

or WMMT is switched on,

vibration connects the whole community

like an aerial view of Whitesburg—

as though God is listening.

Party for Wiley's Girlfriend

Maybe Katy's party was planned too far in advance.

Wiley was more a genius of spontaneity.

His aunt made calls and sent out invitations.

A cousin made the reservations.

Tolly provided festive decorations.

Wiley was assigned one thing—to get the cake.

The night of the party,

Wiley is running late.

When the restaurant staff

encircle with a guitar,

ready to sing, *Happy Birthday*,

his aunt motions to cue Wiley.

Did you forget something? she prompts.

Wiley jumps up,

I'll be right back.

Wiley is gone so long

that speculation sets in—

maybe he was waiting on eggs to be laid

to make the cake from scratch,

maybe he pulled over to write *poultry*,

or got pulled over.

Finally, he returns with a huge cake,

rectangular as the Miss Rhododendron float.

He beams as all behold

the sugary flourish of pastel flowers,

fluffy yellow chicks and cute bunny rabbits—

and the words,

Happy Easter, Claire!

SAWC Gathering at Highlander

A rookie asked Wiley

how he got to be called Ski King.

Wiley started to tell the story,

heard so many times before.

He interrupted himself,

said he had to take stage right,

and walked out of the room.

Giggles trailed him.

Pauletta picked up where Wiley left off.

Dana pitched in a few more details.

Dick was finishing the tale

as Wiley returned to listen to the end.

He stepped inside the circled rocking chairs,

waved his hat off,

I never knew before

that I could go on without myself.

Wiley Tells the History of Highlander

Used to, you could look off this deck.

and see black cars line the entire edge

of that wide field below—

the *FBI*—

because of the carryings on

of subversive activities

like quilting, buck dancing,

and Cherokee basket weaving.

Highlander lets SAWC meet here probably

because we write against mountaintop removal

and don't break anything.

Way back, people for unions

came to learn how to organize.

During the Civil Rights Movement,

Rosa Parks was here.

Martin Luther King Jr.

probably stood on this very spot,

his thoughts fused to these blue mountains—

noble thoughts in mountains still there—

above the black cars directed toward him

like torpedoes.

Highlander Group Photo

(after Wiley's poem about wishing he was taller)

During SAWC's workshop of my poems,

I asked if I should keep the line

I am used to bigger dicks.

Most thought not,

but Wiley said to keep it.

So I kept it

until the poem was about to be published—

when I realized I was not the man

Wiley was.

Gathering for the group photo,

Dick directed me to stand next to him.

No, Dana said, *She's used to, well—*

taller men.

The Delbert Awards at Highlander

A few unsuspecting newcomers
all want to win Rookie of the Year—
and they do.

Jim, Mike, John, and Dick
drum roll on the arms of rocking chairs
until Wiley calls the winner up.
All cheer with great excitement,
Speech! Speech!
The Rookie of the Year begins, *Thank . .*
Scott shouts, *That's enough! Next!*
To that newcomer's surprise,
Wiley calls again, *Now the Rookie of the Year Award*
goes to—drum rolls again.
Then, Owen hands out another
nicely framed certificate
with a Dollar Store trinket,
based on a line from that author's work,
until all the rookies are included.

Once they catch on,
all get a good laugh.
Owen asks them not to give it away
to rookies next year—
for now, they know the secret of our hearts.

Chartreuse

In between sessions at the ASA Conference,

SAWC emerged onto the sidewalk,

staring blank as an unwritten page.

We drank beer from rinsed coffee cups

where no scholar would be suspect

at the edge of university steps.

You're just one of the guys, Scott toasted

his styrofoam against mine,

a fuzzy click.

Dick bought the first bottle of Chartreuse,

duty free, at an airport in Iceland.

Thus, tradition was born at Highlander

to toast with a thimble full, so precious,

of sweet herbs trailing a cold creek.

Smoldering in the throat,

the green taste sets the heart aflame,

blazes through veins until capillaries

dilate into tender leaves beneath skin

cooled by night air.

Dick explains the liqueur's green color—

made by Carthusian monks since the 1700s.

A story from far away becomes ours.

I can feel all our stories of Appalachia

fall into place

as we stand together.

I look around.

We are one spirit—

the swarpers and the swarpettes,

not just one of the guys,

but one of us.

Poultry in Motion

So a feather, really, is just a spark to ignite the air.
My god of all wrinkled mountains, I can't wait to fly again.

—Jim Minick, "Cicero on Feathers"

Anytime you put poison in your water source, it's a kind of crazy
thing to do. It's an aberration. It's evidence of a serious psychic
dislocation, an alienation from the natural world.
It's nest fouling is what it is.

—Gurney Norman, *Headwaters—Gurney Norman* (video)

Yes, the earth / is / the garden, / but this time /
we are the God / throwing / ourselves / out.

—Rhonda Pettit, "Genesis Revised (circa e. 21ˢᵗ C)"

Everyone is a Christ, by any means necessary.
Pick up your own cross and just hold on.

—Omope Carter Daboiku, "3M: Just Posted after 50 Years"

Wiley Quixote Says Grace

He doesn't joust with windmills

but fights for them to replace coal.

He dislikes being called Wiley Coyote

and *Appalachian* rhymed with *station,*

but he laughs when *poetry*

in our mountain dialect

is misunderstood for *poultry.*

In his poem, titled *Poultry,*

he resonates with the chicken yard.

He calls himself a *poult.*

In a world that mostly misunderstands,

calling yourself a poet sounds pretentious.

After all, poetry won't put fried chicken on the table—

but it will feed the soul, Wiley protests.

Wiley has a great voice for GPS,

but we might end up not leaving at all:

You can't get there from here

but seeing you're already here, celebrate!

He can deflect

hurt into humor,

poultry into poetry,

and a mispronounced *App-a-lay-shun*

into a rhyme on his radio station—

we are a part of this nation so get it right!

That's not all he has to say.

Wiley was raised not to take the Lord's name in vain,

but he demands Greedheads stop

their goddamned strip mining

and mountaintop removal now!

Pioneer Stereo

The way Wiley describes
his closeness to his brother
is to tell about the Pioneer stereo.

On furlough from the Army,
Robb bought Wiley a stereo.
Not just any stereo, Wiley emphasizes,
but a Pioneer!

Robb surprised Wiley,
in his dorm room at Berea,
with the sound system
of dreams.

Many times since then,
successful Robb built, reinforced, and rebuilt for Wiley—
provided private nursing after Wiley's broken leg.
Still, this one act of giving—
With his Army money, Wiley still can't get over it.
College life was already good for Wiley,
but just got better.

Robb was facing Vietnam.

Bob Henry Offers an Art Class at the ASA Conference

I am so pleased with my baby food jar

covered with pennies and plastic toys

pressed into tile adhesive—

green army soldier stuck from the side like a handle—

that I involve my young son.

We collect pebbles beside the river

to cover plastic flamingos,

worn albino by the sun.

My son teases me over my enthusiasm

resulting in yard art

too flamboyant

for wire legs to support.

Heavy flamingos lay on their sides along our path.

One eye,

in position to look heavenward,

as with all dying birds

seems to stare with only one question,

America, why hast thou forsaken me?

The Confessional

After the SAWC reading,

Wiley's best friend

walks over to me,

takes my hand,

wends me

down hotel hallways

to his room,

and closes the door.

We do not turn on the light.

We never touch.

We lay on the bed straight as Bic pens.

The ceiling absorbs our words

like a black hole,

never to be voiced again.

All night, our secrets drain the black ink from the window

to refill with violet.

Before I leave,

he wants to tell me one more thing—

that he thinks my poetry is good.

For some, love does not come all at once,

from just one person, but is cumulative.

I accept the gifts I have received from men,

saved for later to unwrap slowly,

like now, with something to offer back.

The Arrow

I asked Wiley what the worst thing

he'd ever done was,

and he had an answer handy.

When I was a young'un,

I shot my Granny in the butt with an arrow.

I wondered if she got mad.

Nah, she was hanging out clothes

knew I was just playing,

and didn't mean it.

Even the worst thing Wiley has done is funny.

That isn't true for everyone.

I think of another Granny when I was growing up—

God-fearing and so good

that you became good around her.

Before she and her husband wed,

she became pregnant.

For that one thing,

she lived her life with the undertow of shame.

Shame is a kind of missing

who we would have been without it.

It rusts from the inside out.

Wiley had the ability not to regret,

not to miss.

Zen Buddhist monks never missed—

so proficient at hitting the target.

Not to waste arrows during practice,

they simply pulled back on the empty bow.

Pink Flamingos in Kentucky

Wiley asks if I have flamingos at home.

He runs under the deck,

comes back with a pink plastic pair,

still in the package with that new record smell.

These are the good ones, Wiley proudly declares,

not the cheap imitation kind.

Rich with beta carotene,

a diet of blue-green algae, shellfish,

and crustaceans

ripens the white flamingo until pink—

the way hydrangea blooms

depend on aluminum sulfate or lime

to adjust the soil pH

that produces pink or blue.

Nevertheless,

a bird of pink curvature

wearing stilt high heels

amid turquoise water

is sheer enchantment—

the same colors of tile

in Wiley's bathroom,

the foyer to his cabin.

After all the fires of global warming,

a future generation might unearth

and marvel, as we did, at the revelry

of plastic flamingos, plucked pink and skewered,

flying weightless in space on thin wires

in Kentucky.

A similar archeological dig

in my yard

might open the small pocket

of pennies and iron nails

where the hydrangea flourished.

I knew it was an old wives' tale,

that planting one or the other among roots

had nothing to do

with my expectant mother's gift

turning pink or blue.

Yet, I hope my love for the smallest single cell

and how everything is electrical—

my love of life—

be understood, somehow, by my indecision

when choosing between any two.

12 Poems

Wiley stops listening

to the poet reading,

upholds his right hand

in allegiance to Pine Mountain.

12 poets,

adjourned,

watch the mustache of the woods

above the gum line of the road,

wide open for the rotten smile

of a   coal-laden   18-wheeler

put on pause

before its descent

into breaking the law

that bans big trucks from this blind-curve road

to promote school bus safety.

Wiley springs into action,

It's 2:56 pm on July 27, 2001—write that down!

12 poets with 12 pieces of paper

glare into the immortal white

of standing up against mountain range removal

and the frick and frack of gas.

The wind speaks in the tongue of laurel.

12 poets with cool pens in hand,

as best they can,

write it—

gears shifting,

grinding,

going

down

in flames.

Wiley Says He'll Never Write a Novel

When his "Get In, Jesus" poem

was published in a college text,

Wiley was able to take a whole year

just to write.

Leaving a honky tonk,

he rested his notebook

on the roof of his car.

He drove off, and the notebook slipped

into the dimension where lost things go.

His main canon went up in flames

in the first fire

and he could not recreate

what memory burned with grief.

Scott collected what remained

from notebooks, paper plates, napkins, publications,

and the *Appalachian Journal*

where Jerry Wayne's drawer was left intact

over a decade after his retirement.

Jesus never wrote anything,

not even the Gospels.

He had people to do that for him.

Wiley likes the act of writing—

his computer still in a box.

Girlfriends typed his first publications.

Like Jesus, he never learned

how to type or hang glide.

Music to Life

At the top of the Whirled,

Pine Mountain Sand and Gravel Company

stamped its mark,

open and barren in the forest.

I ask Wiley if he thinks

there should be music to life.

He gasps, *Isn't there?*

I mean like in the movies.

It would help us know what to expect.

A drum beat would warn

if a nefarious character lurks

with a hidden knife and a plan.

A lovely piano trill

would let us know when love is mutual.

Wiley wonders what should be playing now,

amid the orange and redolent swirls of sand,

dubbed MARS by Wiley.

Rhapsody in Blue, I suggest, *by Gershwin.*

He agrees though he stands

on the site of rock concerts.

As we head back to the Sand Bar(d) Gorilla,

he says, *Anything John Prine about now.*

Of course, there is music to his life

because of the concerts he hosts,

ants busy as musical notes in the sand,

and branches that conduct the wind.

Years later, on the deck at Highlander—

at the edge of a bowl of mountains and valley below—

I can't take my eyes off the panoramic view.

Wiley stops as he goes by,

I reckon you're enjoying the fiddle tune

in the music to life.

Goose Creek Symphony

Reba and I used to sing Goose Creek Symphony songs

while we swept, washed dishes, hoed, walked,

and dreamed of being famous singers.

All the while, Bandana Creek played along.

The air, cooler with spearmint, along its bank

projected our imagination far enough then

to meet up with us now.

Our band name, facetiously, would be

called Bandana Creek.

Wiley was once a roadie for Goose Creek Symphony.

Twenty years after my first book was published

at a street concert of GCS in Johnson City,

I gave Richie Hart a copy of *Bandana Creek*—

explained the origin of the title.

I told him I knew Wiley Quixote.

He had that same smile everyone has

when they fast-forward the antics of Wiley.

He said, *Ah, you'll be alright.*

Unlike Greedheads, Wiley Says He's a Varlet

Once I asked Wiley if he felt the way I did,

that I was ugly, if that was a poet thing.

No, he reflected, *I always thought*

I was a right smart looking feller.

I was always a varlet though.

After our first reading together in 1978,

Wiley asked me what I thought of his poems.

He was surprised, called over Bob Henry,

his cohort in activism.

Hey, she thinks I need to toughen up.

They both laughed in disbelief.

That moment of shame

sinks like a skipping stone in the river.

I can identify how the worn striations of gray

burned my hand with more friction and gravity

than a plain flat stone could possess.

Twenty years later, Wiley remembers

and asks me to explain because it hurt him.

I remember.

I thought he needed to edit more.

He asks if I would help him with that

because I am his favorite poet.

You tell all the poults that, I jeer.

You're right, he admits.

I'm a varlet.

Wiley Says He Doesn't Want to Be Tied Down

Wiley will not be tied down today,

not when birds give a wake-up call

with notes lighter than helium balloons.

His wrists will not be bound

with worn bandanas,

so tight that bruises

could be mistaken

for the gathering storm.

He will not be gagged

but speak for the Appalachian people,

their mountains eviscerated.

Not today, not this day,

his attention settles like fog

on a fir twig here, a laurel spray there.

At his iron flamingo gate,

Wiley is not a world traveler.

He could have been a famous actor,

but he chose to stay

and help his people.

He feels the hollowness of his holler,

the last place to gather sunrise

and the first to lose the sunset.

Between that gauzy space

of not wanting to be tied down

and responsible stewardship of his last resort,

the lines of his own poetry

seem to rope him down.

All the Poets Are Not Asleep

When rest comes to the weary
it arrives on the coattails of momentum
and poems written in the chaos of 3am . . .
and the escapades of loose, bellowing hounds
on the scent outside curtainless windows . . .
in private drives on holler roads.

—Kelli Hansel Haywood, "Autumn Equinox, 3am"

At four-fourteen, a cat,
made nervous by the wind,
leaves its hidden place.
The nighthawk gathers the last of its moths
and goes to nest.

—Michael Henson, "Lightning at Four-Twenty-Nine:
    A Poem for Aralee Strange"

. . . the Pleiades
and I are keeping company with wind
and moon and all the timelessness of dark
and stars and my provisioned heart.

—Dana Wildsmith, *Christmas in Bethlehem*

Good night, bright strangers, I love that you assail
the darkness we are all trapped in as if light were imminent.

—Ron Houchin, "Flowers at Night"

I am trying to believe it is not the weight,
but how we carry what we're given that bends
us down, or lets us float awhile, suspended
in these years between the gathering up
and letting go.

—Pauletta Hansel, "Postcard from Age 60"

Wiley's Silver Cap in My Lap

Turtle shell empty of gravity,

a deflated moon,

holds more light

than anything

in the dark auditorium.

Wiley Goes to the Highest Peak

White,

so much white—

Wiley's jeep zips

a polka-dot dress of white trillium

up the back of Black Mountain.

He pulls over,

steps out into the view—

mountains, pew after pew, face God.

In comparison, it is heartbreaking to discern

the next ridge that has timber,

felled, haphazard as Pick-Up Sticks.

Nearby, demolished mountainsides

are covered with a chemical blue—

the equivalent of Milk of Magnesia's

eerie pink if it were blue.

Unconvincing as an old TV commercial

of a bald head undergoing spray paint to feign hair,

the first rain will funnel this seed paint

into gullies with debris ricocheting

down a bowling alley for striking out

the valley below.

The top of Black Mountain is black.

Coal extraction creates a moonscape

too filthy for an American flag.

The coal company has staked its claim

in black and white,

with a grubby "Do Not Litter" sign,

the candle on the cake of Wiley's disgust.

Wiley Flees Coal Company Security

Wiley's Last Resort is on the second-highest peak

in Kentucky, and Wiley wants to keep it that way,

but the only thing

holding up Black Mountain

as the highest peak is a cell tower.

Otherwise, the coal company would have

scraped that away too.

Jeff climbs out to photograph the *Do Not Litter* sign—

black lettering on a white sign on black ground

as far as he can see.

Color film has no choice but to develop in black and white.

He jumps back into the jeep

as a security truck

darts toward them like a wasp.

Wiley speeds off

down the wrong side of the mountain—

no time to turn around and head back home.

In full pursuit,

the truck chases them all the way

into another county

and towns of rock buildings

crafted by Italian stonemasons

seduced into coming to this country for work,

only to end up in the mines.

After quick turns onto backroads,

Wiley finally shakes off the wasp.

They howl into the wind of their escape.

What would the coal company do to them?

They don't want to know.

They notice that in nearly every yard they pass,

a trampoline stands, black as a miner's lung.

They start to count them.

Then they notice the aboveground pools

and count them too.

A long way back to Wiley's,

they lose count at dusk

when trampolines and pools dilate

to become the darkness

they wish they had never seen.

Wiley's Heart Is in the Right Place

After the SAWC reading at ASA,

Wiley came up to me

because, as a nurse,

I represent all healthcare.

The hospital hoodooed me,

he complained. *They charged me $40*

for an aspirin, then ran all kinds of tests

I didn't even need

and charged me for them too.

Wasn't nothing wrong, he lamented, *except my heart.*

I had already learned through the grapevine

about his arrhythmia.

I began to ponder Wiley's heart—

loved by countless friends and women,

rarely alone, his campfire forever circled

by those who enjoy an adult beverage

in a dry county on their way home.

Some are already there in a camper for the season.

Some see the fire from the road

and drop by to catch up.

The flames sway like a chorus, harmoniously changing—

maybe a banjo picker, filmmaker, and hairdresser

are joined by someone asking for directions.

The next hour, nearly all have left

except for the newly arrived guitarist and waitress.

Stories, music, jokes

are directed toward a fire

that holds its own against the darkness.

Wiley must have felt alone sometimes—

St. John's Wort on a medicine shelf,

a world beating chaotic

as the chambers of his heart.

From his bed those nights

before confronting insurance

or coal companies in court,

he must have watched limbs

sword fight outside his window.

He must have felt

that all the poets are asleep.

Note to Wiley

Against the orange sunset

between Snake and Rich Mountains,

and a hand's breadth above the nearest tree line,

a loud cricket dreams the hardest of all

about ancient conifers.

My small son used to swing hard on my arms.

I would tell him I was not a tree,

and the memory pierces me now

as the cricket stirs my soul

with the former ebullience of my grown son.

Between the sky and the reflection of sky on lakes,

canoes skimmed toward us like loose tongues

of an invisible foe.

Whole cultures were swallowed up.

All that is left to cherish

is the cool wind remainder

of what was once a virgin forest.

We never admitted this—

that dimension

is what we love the most about the mountains—

a green ridge slanting in front of another

and the one behind that leaning in the opposite direction,

and beyond, a succession

from green to purple to dark blue into lighter blues.

The dimension of how sound carries delights us—

a current of leaves rustling below the path to feign a creek

and the Tweetsie whistle, a 45-minute drive away,

heard from my deck in Sugar Grove.

Across the river

a rooster greets my morning

from its yard, a tiny square,

smaller than on a Monopoly board.

I toast my cup of coffee

to one birdhouse from another.

Dear Poet Brother,

I know you understand what this means to me.

I breathe this information to you.

Wiley Attends Hindman Writers' Workshop at Night

Wednesday night is chicken 'n' dumplings,

the hardest night for dish duty

which doesn't affect Wiley.

He has been banned from Hindman—

something about an adult beverage on campus.

Now, everyone knows to drink from a Dixie cup

and only after Mike Mullins and his staff go home.

Wiley is allowed, though, to attend evening readings,

open to the public.

Wednesday is the big reading night,

and tonight is Silas,

who camped out his first time here.

Wiley likes his activism, wants him to do well,

and has interviewed him on WMMT.

Wiley, known here as the Ski King,

sweeps across campus like a slow avalanche

collecting old friends

along the way to the auditorium.

By the time he arrives,

an entourage trails him like a long robe.

Afterwards, there's singing

and Dixie cups abound.

George Ella, Rita, and Les strum their guitars.

Joyce joins in on the banjo.

Jane knows all the words to the hymns

but passes out copies of the lyrics.

The pretty voices of Dana and Marianne stand out.

Sherry looks and sounds like an angel.

After a short pause to gather refreshments,

Jason leads us into, "I'll Fly Away."

Linda and Leatha quickly end their conversation

and move closer in.

Gurney closes his eyes and listens

to the music of all his life.

Wiley and Ron Houchin,

partners in poultry,

continue to laugh and talk

on the periphery of the porch railing.

Before time to settle down,

we stand holding hands in a large circle

and sing the prayer of

"Now Is the Cool of the Day,"

to open the Jim Wayne Miller

annual memorial reading of "The Briar."

Each steps up to the mic,

reads a couple lines of "The Briar"

visible by flashlight.

The night expands

from the dark edge of a book

on life and death.

Jim Wayne Miller is here.

He is really here

in the lightning bugs

released by his words

in the cool swim of mountain air.

Perhaps we already sense it—

the night air that knows everything.

We can know it too

if shaken from the dark.

But we cannot appreciate Wiley more

than we already do

even if we could know

that SAWCers will someday

take turns reading

the "Get In, Jesus" poem.

Vinyl Record

The needle floats over waves to produce sound.

The wind across the pelagic variations

of a long-range mountain view

amplifies a kind of hum, a mantra.

I held new album covers to my heart,

studied every detail of artwork, made drawings

of the musician photos, and memorized lyrics—

active listening while the music played.

Songs, vibrant and abstract, different from anything before,

became a part of my experience, my DNA,

that I passed on to my sons.

I have always seen the music in their movement—

drawing with crayons or running past me.

I could not explain a vinyl record to a caveman.

I still cannot get over fire.

The scientific explanation falls short

of the music that sails across a flat world,

sometimes falling off.

The way sound got in there, the way it gets out

is magic.

I cannot explain sound

or my mother playing piano, her self-taught ragtime style.

She recorded with gospel groups on those thick 78s

that my young brother tossed as a Frisbee

across the fields and shadows of loss.

Sometimes the record, held slant,

reveals a blackberry patch of scratches.

Sometimes it breaks its own habit

over and over a deep line,

fixing itself,

even as I am on my way

to the rescue.

In the recording studio,

two sound waves that hit head-on

cancel each other out—

no sound at all, a dead spot.

Wiley Quixote promoted Appalachian musicians and poets,

broadcast on his WMMT show,

Ridin' Around Listenin' to the Radio.

From the control room,

he would switch on the intercom in the office

to request a CD or something else forgotten,

Is anyone there? he would ask.

Interns, fondly tittering, would reply, *No.*

No sound at all is hard to comprehend—

that one sound plus one sound can equal zero.

Live and let live! Wiley proclaimed

across frequencies

that practice the same cursive exercise

as the Blue Ridge Mountains,

fading dark blue until lighter and lighter

into the light blue sky,

ringing outward forever.

Wiley's Cache

When Wiley was eight, he worked

a few days at his uncle's company,

Pine Mountain Sand and Gravel.

Wiley said his job was shouting at truck drivers,

Hey, we need more sand!

Really, he declared, *I worked at doing nothing.*

At the end of the week,

he waited in line to get paid

alongside men,

hyphenated by metal lunch buckets.

An official company check

with the company logo—

Don't worry about the mule going blind,

just load the wagon—

was made out to him for $10.56.

It may as well have been ten million

to the suspended disbelief

of the dangling office light bulb.

Wiley never cashed the check,

sacred as the perfect marijuana leaf

pressed between his favorite lines

of "Ode to a Nightingale."

(The local sheriff's department found it,

but that's another story. Let's just say Road Hog

was in the garden and graciously took the fall.)

He framed the check.

Nothing the check could buy

could be better than the check itself.

Eventually,

heirloom furniture, photos, and the check

inside his family home

went up in flames—

in what became known as

The First Fire.

It's not so hard to picture Heaven where parents go—

a quiet spring dotted with Lily of the Valley.

But where do beloved objects go?

After a fire, absence formed by cremation,

could there be a place where a stuffed lamb

might be rewarded for its own brand of being good,

allowed to leap through infinite buttercup fields

just for the sake of how deeply it was loved?

Conversely, is there not a burning locus of justice

designated for a big coal company

that allegedly likes to play with fire?

There must be a place, a special Heaven,

for Wiley's Pine Mountain Sand and Gravel check,

where it could rise from ashes.

Its symbol of brotherly love

could flutter in wind

entrusted for a magic carpet ride.

The check could forever monitor

a place like these mountains used to be,

dripping with wild grapes and clear cataracts—

devoid of moonscape mines,

their deep riches never burnt out.

The Lyrebird

Twenty stories high—

Wiley recalled traffic held up

as the monster dragline

crossed the highway.

Before the dragline

claws away the mountaintop

to smother the dreams of valleys,

there is the chainsaw.

There are the fires—

no time to harvest the timber

in the rush to get the coal.

I cannot get Wiley's line out of my mind,

buzzsaws in the rain,

or the intimations of the Lyrebird—

its rainforest,

like our Appalachian mountains,

becoming extinct.

Miniature recording studio with wings,

the Lyrebird's cover songs

are so impressive

that other species are fooled

and drop by to go courting.

Amidst this lovely repertoire,

he bolts out an exact rendition

of the disturbing brattle of a chainsaw.

I want to hold this bird,

a toddler taught to curse,

to heal such visceral gnawing

until replaced

by the call of a whippoorwill—

what connects our souls to the cool of night.

Even as chainsaws butchered the rain,

dilated pupils of umbrellas

searched the above

and a precious bird

sang deep within Wiley.

Travel Mugs

I. Wiley Leaves Another One Behind

I was already grateful for the red mug

I knew he would forget

the last time he rode in my car

to and from his last ASA conference.

Back home, I found it upright,

tucked behind the rib cage of my bags.

His DNA clinging to the portal,

the dark smell of coffee etched inside.

I peered into its black hole.

Diagnosed with pancreatic cancer—

gone the next week.

Poet brother and hero of Appalachia,

the look of agony on his face was true.

He left his 80-acre campground and lake

for the community to enjoy.

Once again, he made an entrance

with everything he had

and left something tangible behind.

II. My Brother's Silver Mug Is Shaped Like a Bullet

I cannot sit another second on Kim's porch

where he shot himself last night.

I walk around the magical house he built—

how he felled poplars to strip the bark for siding,

carved laurel handles for wormy chestnut cabinets,

and made Christmas tree cut-outs in shutters.

He paid his employees more than he made himself.

In spiked grass below the porch,

his travel mug lies inert

as a fish long out of water.

Despite its stiff smell of vodka,

this is the one

Kim drank coffee from every morning,

now empty.

III. The One I Carry Is Not Whole

It has gone the way of so many others—

lid lost, no longer able to fully serve its purpose.

After people die,

they become invisible

in the clothes of our memory.

Wiley forever wears his silver cap and gold jacket.

My brother, in jeans and work boots,

might say, *End this poem already.*

His pain was greater than his care

for my struggle to rest on a positive note.

I could tell one of his jokes

except for my bad timing and elusive punch line.

There's nothing good to say

when I've lost brothers,

when America has lost brothers—

beautiful, beautiful brothers.

Direction spun like a bottle,

I carry on.

There's no good way to end.

Five Words

In the last video of Wiley Quixote,

just out of the hospital with pneumonia

but congenial as ever,

his breath is labored.

He would have laughed

if told he had SOB,

the old medical shorthand

for shortness of breath.

He becomes the pivot

of Appalachian music, campers, and the creek

there, in the background.

He treats the interviewer

the way he treats everyone—

as the most important person on Earth.

Asked if he will come back next year,

his answer, *Definitely*,

stills our hearts.

When asked to describe the festival

in five words,

he is delighted.

A man of words,

a man of his word,

he counts out the words

that spring from fingertips

on one tremulous hand.

He counts.

We count on him.

No years left for him to count

in these hallowed hollers,

he speaks for us all:

Let the mountains ring forever.

Wiley Came In and Went Out with the Hunter's Moon

At Wiley's bedside

in the cabin by Walled-in Pond,

I said, *It's me, your favorite poet.*

He managed a smile

and carefully prepared the words,

That's right.

Wiley didn't think he was good enough

to ask God why He had forsaken him.

He had asked why America

would destroy the mountains and betray its people.

He didn't ask for medication to ease his suffering.

He thought he deserved the pain.

In his "Get In, Jesus" poem,

crazed drunks mock the hitchhiker,

What's it like dying on the cross?

There is exhaustion before asphyxiation.

There is thirst.

Jesus was offered vinegar

on a cloth tied to a stick.

Wiley accepted a red Popsicle

with gratitude.

Eyes fixed and Cheyne-Stokes respirations,

it was time, I felt, for him and Katy to be alone.

That night, the Hunter's Moon was bigger

than the moon could be—

huge fist against the night.

I wondered if Wiley might be

on that barren landscape,

made familiar by mountaintop removal.

He might take respite there—

to celebrate his view of what's left

of Earth's green and blue

and to plan a soiree for other layover souls,

before that one giant leap into forever—

the moon as Wiley's *last resort.*

Footnote to Wiley's Last Resort

Annual Pine Mountain Tacky Lawn Ornament and Pink Flamingo Soiree: Since 1985, during the full moon in August, this weekend swarp of continuous poetry readings and band performances around the clock takes place at Wiley's Last Resort. Attendees decorate their campsites overzealously to compete for the prize—that they have to take. Solar Christmas lights, pink flamingos, signage, sculpture, bizarre hats and dress, homemade wine and other libations abound. At midnight, all music stops. All is quiet until Wiley gives the cue to howl in unison at the moon.

Appalachian Studies Association Conference (ASA): An annual conference held at different universities in Appalachia consisting of a group of scholars, teachers, and regional activists who believe their shared community will continue to be important to the writing, researching, and teaching about Appalachia.

Appalachian Voices: Jim Webb served on the Board of Directors for this non-profit, grassroots, community advocate founded in 1997. Appalachian Voices brings people together to protect the land, air, and water of Central and Southern Appalachia and advance a just transition to a generative and equitable clean energy economy. Their newspaper is called *The Appalachian Voice.*

Appalshop: Multimedia cultural arts organization in Whitesburg, Kentucky, serving Southeast Kentucky communities for over 40 years. WMMT Radio is housed under the auspices of Appalshop.

Delbert Awards: Humorous event on Saturday night of SAWC gathering at Highlander. Based on lines from a writer's work or something spoken, certificates and trinkets purchased from the Dollar Store are presented.

Highlander Research and Education Center: Since 1932, Highlander has provided social justice leadership training and served as a cultural center in New Market, Tennessee.

Hindman Settlement School: Provides educational services for dyslexic children and their parents, manages community service programs to promote cultural heritage and growth, including the annual Writers' Workshop.

MARS: Former sand quarry. Acronym for Music, Art, Re-creation, Sustainability, MARS Fest began in 2008 on Pine Mountain at Wiley's Last Resort as a showcase for local and regional musicians, artists, writers, and folks who care about the preservation, perpetuation, and promotion of Appalachian music, art, culture, and life.

Pine Mountain Sand & Gravel (*PMS&G*): Annual publication of the Southern Appalachian Writers Cooperative, whose mission is to encourage, support, and publicize the work of members and friends. Founding editor: Jim Webb. Founding Publisher: Robb Webb.

Poult: One who writes poetry.

Poultry: Poetry, mispronounced when someone either hears this word instead of *poetry* or is making fun of poets and poetry.

SAWCer (*sawr kər*): A member of the Southern Appalachian Writers Cooperative.

Seedtime on the Cumberland: An annual festival held by Appalshop in Whitesburg, Kentucky. Seedtime features many aspects of mountain life, including music, arts, crafts, dance, writing, filmmaking, and much more. It is a celebration of the artistry of mountain people.

Ski King: AKA Jim Webb.

Southern Appalachian Writers Cooperative (SAWC): Co-founded by Jim Webb, Gurney Norman, Peggy Dotson Hall, and Ron Short in 1974, SAWC supports and encourages writers who identify with the Appalachian culture. The group continues to meet annually to workshop and swarp at Highlander Center, Hindman Settlement School, Appalachian Studies Association, and Wiley's Last Resort.

Swarp: This word is distinctly Appalachian for drinking and acting the fool. In the nature of SAWC, a swarp includes jesting without hurting anyone's feelings. That's not what we do. However, there might be a jar of moonshine passed around.

Swarper: In context with this book, one who swarps at a SAWC event or at Wiley's Last Resort.

Swarpetta: Pauletta Hansel.

Swarpette: Endearment for a female Swarper.

Wiley's Last Resort: Jim Webb's primitive campground that includes over 80 acres and his uncle's former Pine Mountain Sand and Gravel Company. On the top of Pine Mountain, the second highest peak in Kentucky, with only the cell tower on neighboring Black Mountain still maintaining the highest peak.

Wiley Quixote: Jim Webb's alter ego began in his comments in the TVRC's newspaper. He was a character from Webb's play, *Elmo's Haven*. Later, the persona developed into a radio show of Webb's on WMMT, called "Ridin' Around Listenin' to the Radio with Wiley Quixote."

WMMT-FM: Radio station, owned by Appalshop and housed upstairs in the Appalshop building in Whitesburg, Kentucky, has the mission to be a 24-hour voice of mountain people's music, culture, and social issues; to provide broadcast space for creative expression and community involvement in making radio; and to be an active participant in discussion of public policy that will benefit coalfield communities and the Appalachian region as a whole. Jim Webb was semi-retired from his work there as a radio personality.

Works Cited

Baber, Bob Henry. "Heirs." *A Picture From Life's Other Side.* 1994. Print.

Duboiku, Omope Carter. "3M: Just Posted after 50 years." *Pine Mountain Sand & Gravel.* Volume 17, 2014.

Goebel, Scott. "Remembering Founding Publisher Robb Webb." *Pine Mountain Sand & Gravel.* Volume 24, 2021.

Congo, Paul. Producer. *Headwaters - Gurney Norman.* Video. Appalshop Archive. Sept. 10, 2010. youtube.comwatch?v=FRKYYZE8V4s. May 2.

Ginsberg, Allen. "Howl." *Poetry Foundation.* poetryfoundation. org/poems/49303/howl. May 10, 2022.

Gipe, Robert. "Re: Wiley's Last Resort." Email to Hilda Downer. May 27, 2022.

Hague, Richard. "Talking Together." *Appalachian Journal.* Volume 24. Summer, 1997.

Hague, Richard. "Dispatch From Wiley's Last Resort." *Appalachian Journal.* Volume 46. Fall, 2018/ Winter, 2019.

Hampton, David Wayne. "Whiskey or Wine." Email to Hilda Downer. May 10, 2022.

Hansel, Pauletta. "Postcard from Age 60." *Heartbreak Tree.* Lake Dallas, Texas: Madville Co., 2022.

Haywood, Kelli Hansel. "Autumn Equinox, 3am." *Pine Mountain Sand & Gravel.* Volume 23, 2020.

Henson, Michael. "The Elements of Sacrifice." *Pine Mountain Sand & Gravel.* Volume 10, 2003.

Henson, Michael. "Lightning at Four-Twenty-Nine: A Poem for Aralee Strange." *Pine Mountain Sand & Gravel.* Volume 17, 2014.

Houchin, Ron. "Ron Houchin - Four Poems." *The Galway Review*. Aug. 13, 2016. thegalwayreview.com/2016/08/13/ron-houchin-four-poems. June 1, 2022.

Miller, Jim Wayne. "Three Days of Rain." *New Ground*. Edited by Donald Askins, David Morris. Jenkins, KY, and White Oak, WV: Southern Appalachian Writers Cooperative and Mountain Review, 1977.

Minick, Jim. "Cicero on Feathers." *Pine Mountain Sand & Gravel*. Volume 17, 2014.

Pendarvis, Edwina. "Appalachian Aubade #2." *Wind*. Issue 88, 2002.

Pettit, Rhonda. "Genesis Revised (circa e. 21st C)." *Pine Mountain Sand & Gravel*. Volume 21, 2018.

Shurgin, Ann. "First Night in a New Bed." *While the Whippoorwill Called*. Hickory, NC: Redhawk Publications, 2022.

Wendell, Berry. The Selected Poems of Wendell Berry. Berkeley: Counterpoint P., 1998.

Wildsmith, Dana. *Christmas in Bethlehem*. Future Cycle Press, 2013.

Bibliography

Staff. "Chamber Spotlights Wiley's Last Resort." *The Mountain Eagle.* Whitesburg: Aug. 19, 2009.

Webb, Jim. "Get In, Jesus." *Literature: The Power of Language.* McLaughlin, Thomas, Editor. San Diego, New York, Chicago, Austin, London, Sydney, Tokyo, Toronto, Washington, D.C.: Harcourt Brace Jovanich Pub., !989.

Webb, Jim. *"Get In, Jesus: New and Selected Poems."* Edited by Scott Goebel. Nicholasville: Wind Publications, 2013.

Wilson, Malcolm. *Jim Webb Kickin' It on the Creek Interview: Let the Mountains Ring Forever!* Video. Irvine: YouTube, 2018.

Wilson, Malcom. *Jim Webb Tribute.* Video. YouTube. Nov. 1, 2018.

Author's Special Thanks

Thank you to those who read the manuscript in its rawness and encouraged me, especially since we are all still under the throes of sadness from the loss of Jim Webb; Sharman and Jeff Chapman-Crane, Scott Goebel, Dick Hague, and Ann Shurgin (also for her editing expertise and moral support). Thank you to all SAWC members who have participated in workshopping some of these poems, especially for their good nature to appear in poems by first name: Bob Henry Baber, Dana Wildsmith, Pauletta Hansel, Richard Hague, Gurney Norman, Sherry Cook Stanforth, Michael Henson, Jim Minick, Owen Cramer, Scott Goebel, Beto Cumming, David Wayne Hampton, Marianne Worthington, Rita Quillen, George Ella Lyon, Jane Hicks, Leatha Kendrick, Beto Cumming, Linda Parsons, Jason Howard, Silas House, John Ray, Les Brown, Joyce Brown, Ann Shurgin, and the late Jim Hinsdale. Robert Gipe, thank you for the lagniappe of sending me your illustration of the book cover without my even asking. Thank you to Jerry Wayne Williamson for publishing both Jim and me and inviting us to read together so long ago. Thank you, Katy Eagle and Steven Justice, for your goodwill during this project, for keeping the resort alive, and for your love of Jim. Thank you to Patty Thompson and editors: Robert Canipe, Tim Peeler, and Aurora Brianna King at Redhawk for your invaluable expertise and support. Scott Goebel is in a league of his own for my appreciation—from his organizing and promoting Jim's work to his scholarly contribution in bringing Appalachian writers to light, providing photographs and clarification of facts, and being there when I doubted myself about details concerning this book.

Previously published by Hilda Downer

Bandana Creek. Red Clay Press, 1979.

Sky Under the Roof. Bottom Dog Press, 2013.

When Light Waits for Us. Main Street Rag Publishing Company, 2021.

Jim visits friends in Cincinatti, 2014.
Photo by Scott Goebel.

About the Author

Hilda Downer is the author of three collections of poetry. Her second book, *Sky Under the Roof,* was a Nautilus Golden Poetry Winner. She retired from teaching English at Appalachian State University as an adjunct while also working as a psychiatric nurse. She has an MFA from Vermont College, and her love of teaching poetry has been fulfilled as a volunteer in local elementary schools. She is a longtime member of the Southern Appalachian Writers Cooperative, the Appalachian Studies Association, and the North Carolina Writers Conference. One of the most important things about her is that she grew up in Bandana of Mitchell County, NC, and has two sons—one a professional fiddler, and the other a visual artist/photographer. She lives in Sugar Grove, North Carolina.

www.ingramcontent.com/pod-product-compliance
Lightning Source LLC
Chambersburg PA
CBHW071126090426
42736CB00012B/2019